4. FOUR LEGS & FOUR FEET

Text by Barbara Cooper

Illustrations by Maggie Raynor

Series consultant: Valerie Watson

Compass Equestrian

© Compass Equestrian Limited 1996
Setting by HRJ
Origination by Dot Gradations
Printed in England by Westway Offset
ISBN 1 900667 03 7

British Library Cataloguing in Publication Data.
A catalogue record for this book is available from the British Library.

When a baby pony, or foal, is born his legs are nearly as long as those of his mother. He has to learn to stand up, then walk, then run, a few hours after he comes into the world. This happens so that if his mother has to run from danger he can keep up with her.

A pony's four legs, like your two legs, have a great deal of work to do, and they take a lot of knocks. When you fall and cut your knee or bruise your shins you can burst into tears or yell or shout "ouch!"

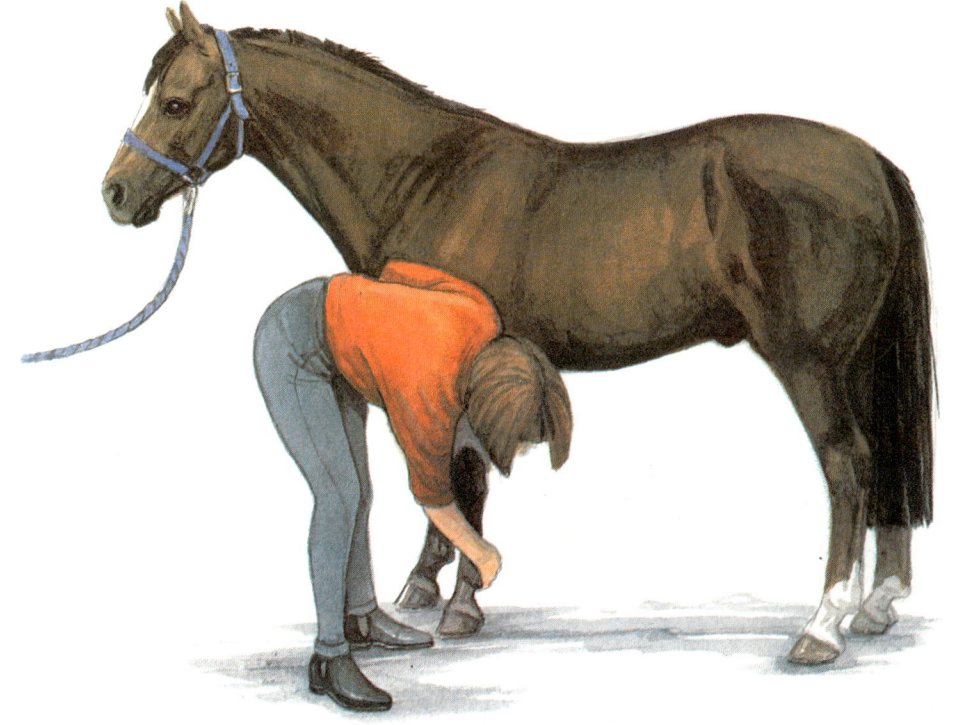

When a pony is hurt he keeps quiet about it : so to make sure that his legs have nothing wrong with them (such as lumps, bumps or cuts), you have to check them carefully every day.

His front legs, or forelegs, are shaped quite differently from his back, or hind, legs. Halfway down his forelegs are his knees, which are made up of seven small bones, like your wrists.

This is how the forelegs should be shaped

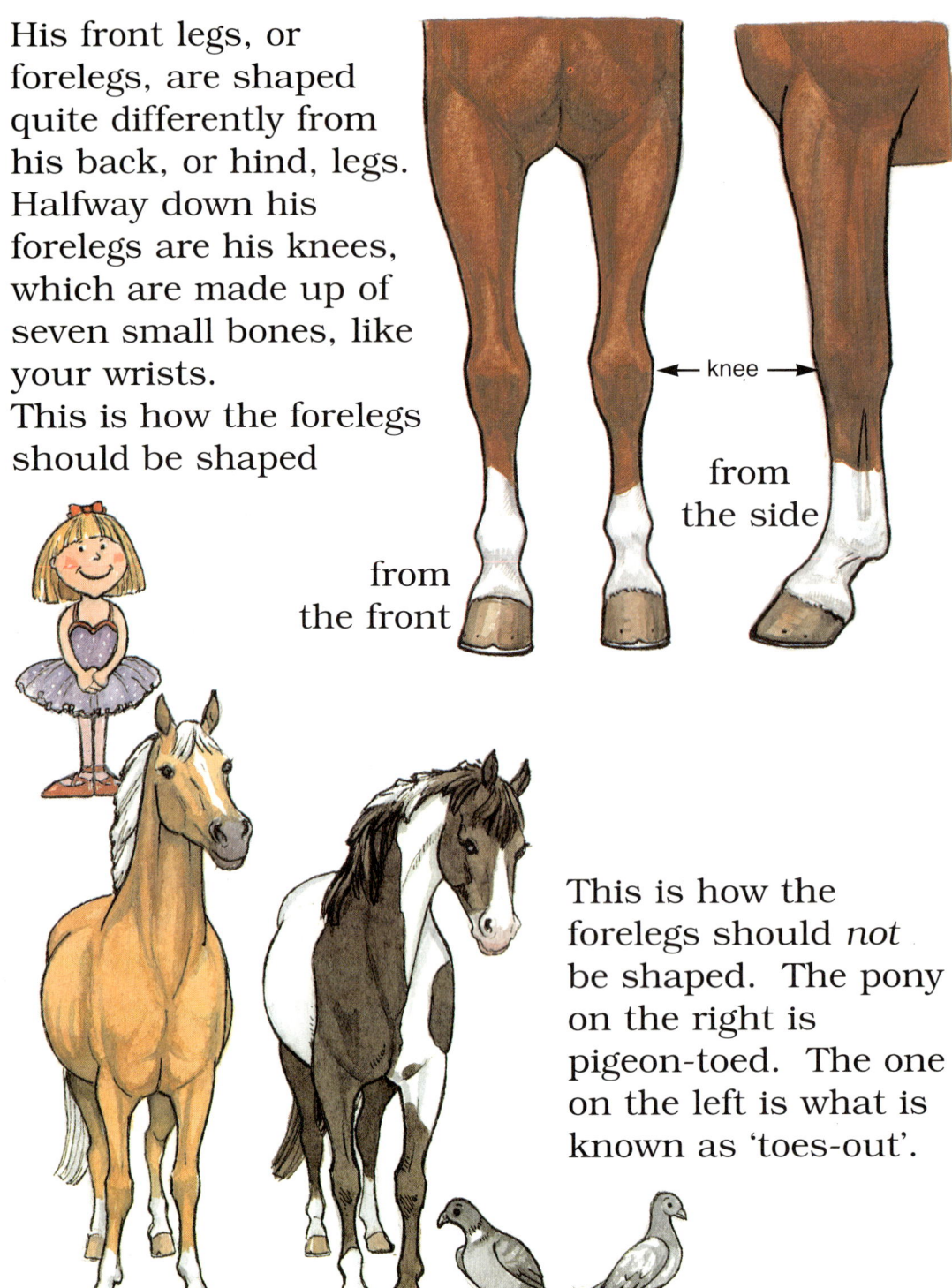

← knee →

from the side

from the front

This is how the forelegs should *not* be shaped. The pony on the right is pigeon-toed. The one on the left is what is known as 'toes-out'.

4

Halfway down his hind legs are what look like pointed, back-to-front knees. They are called 'hocks'. The drawing on the right shows how the hind legs should be shaped

The drawing below shows how the hind legs should *not* be shaped. The pony on the right has 'cow hocks'. The one on the left has 'bowed hocks'.

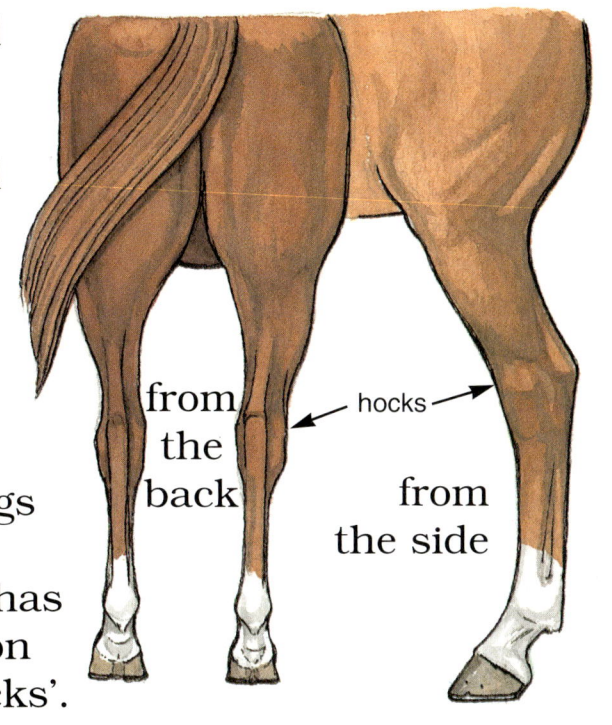

from the back

hocks

from the side

tendon ⟶ ⟵ cannon bone

⟵ fetlock

⟵ pastern

Below his knees and his hocks are his cannon bones, and below his cannon bones are his ankles, called 'fetlocks'. Stretching behind his knees and hocks and down to his fetlocks are strong sinews, like thick cords, which are called 'tendons'.

At the back of his knees a pony has a little bone which comes in very useful when he decides to have a snooze without lying down. The bone locks his knee joints, so his legs don't fold up under him and he is able to sleep standing up.

6

The narrowest part of a pony's leg is the strong, springy joint called the 'pastern', which links the fetlock to the foot. It should slope at a gentle angle.

Too upright, too short.

Too long, too sloping.

Just right.

A pony with well-shaped pasterns, like the one on the left, will give you a smooth, comfortable ride. The pony on the right, with short, upright pasterns, would be likely to give you a bumpy ride, and would probably jar his legs.

A pony can do all kinds of things with his legs,
especially when you are on his back and guiding
him. He can walk backwards, forwards, and
sideways, trot, canter, gallop, jump, buck, turn on a
circle (as on these two pages.) He can even 'skip'!

Some ponies have markings on their legs and fetlocks which help you to recognise them easily. When the hair between the hoof and the fetlock is white, this is called a sock.
When there is white hair from the hoof halfway up the leg it is called a stocking.
A little cluster of black hairs on a white sock just above the hoof is called an 'ermine' mark because it looks like the ermine fur on capes worn by kings and queens.

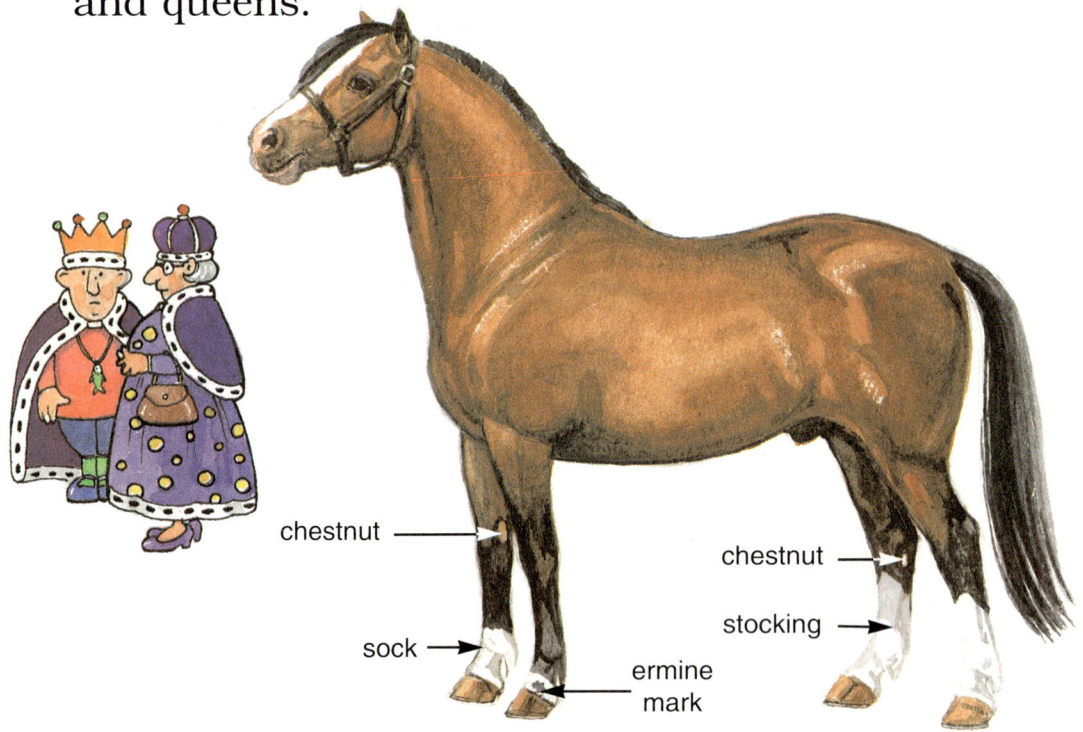

chestnut

chestnut

stocking

sock

ermine mark

All ponies and horses have a marking which looks like a large, horny wart. It can be found on the inside of the forelegs above the knees, and on the hind legs below the hocks. It is called a 'chestnut' and no-one is sure why it is there or what it is for.

A pony's feet, or hooves, are made to match his legs, so his front ones, or forefeet, are a slightly different shape from his back ones, or hind feet.

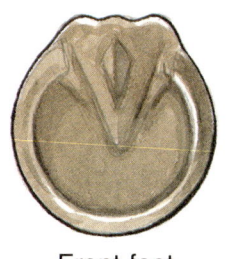

Front foot

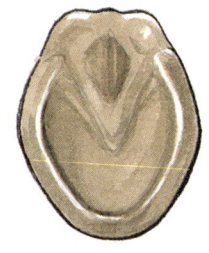

Back foot

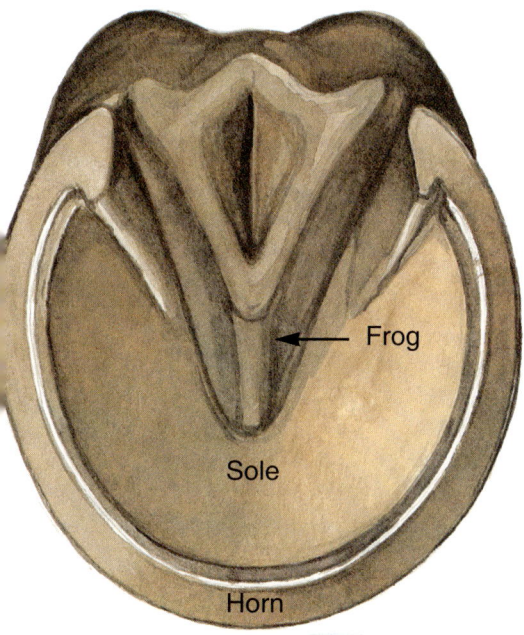

Frog

Sole

Horn

All four feet have a hard covering made of horn, like your nails. When you look at the underneath part, or sole, you can see that the horn grows right down and forms a rim around the sole. Across the middle of the sole is a V-shaped rubbery piece of horn known as the 'frog' which is springy like a jumping frog.

Like your finger-and toe-nails, a pony's hooves keep on growing and have to be regularly trimmed and shaped.

11

A pony can do lots of things with his feet.
He can strike and kick with all four hooves to
protect himself.

He can scratch his body,
his cheeks, his ears, and
his whiskery chin.

And he can 'box' with
other ponies.

In winter he will use his forefeet to scrape away snow so that he can find grass to eat.

When he is very bored or wants you to pay attention to him he will paw the ground with his forefeet.

A naughty pony will always put his feet where they are not meant to be such as in his water-bucket.

He can also tread on you if you get in the way!

Feet come in all shapes and sizes, and you can tell quite a lot about a pony by looking at them.

If they are well-shaped and smooth around the edges it means that the pony has been properly fed and looked after all his life.

If his hooves are long at the toes, broken and rough around the edges, it means that he has not been properly cared for.

Ponies who have been born and live in muddy areas often have large, flat, plate-like feet.

Ponies who live where the ground is always hard (such as the one on the right, from West Africa) have narrower, more upright, boxy feet.

Some farriers say that if a pony's feet are a dark grey colour ('black' hooves) they are stronger than those of the ponies whose hooves are a pale yellowish colour ('white' hooves).

A pony's legs and feet are easy to attend to, so there can be no excuses for failing to keep an eye on them every day. They are also easy to groom and to protect from harm when the pony is working.

A pony's mouth, however, is a different matter: far too many riders are ignorant of what goes on inside it. So if you want to be really kind to your pony you should take the trouble to learn as much as you can about this very important part of him, which is described in the next book:

5. A BIT MORE THAN A MOUTH